JOBS

Susan Canizares
Betsey Chessen

SCHOLASTIC

JOBS

Susan Canizares • Betsey Chessen

Scholastic Inc.
New York • Toronto • London • Auckland • Sydney

Acknowledgments
Literacy Specialist: Linda Cornwell
Social Studies Consultant: Barbara Schubert, Ph.D.

Design: Silver Editions
Photo Research: Silver Editions
Endnotes: Jacqueline Smith
Endnote Illustrations: Anthony Carnabucia

Photographs: Cover: NASA; p. 1: R. Lord/The Image Works; p. 2: Bonnie Kamin/Photo Edit; p. 3: Tom Tracy/Tony Stone Images; p. 4: Tony Freeman/Photo Edit; p. 5: Burns/Monkmeyer Press; pp. 6–7: MacDonald/Envision; p. 8: Larry Lefever/Grant Heilman Photography; p. 9: Charles Gupton/Tony Stone Images; p. 10: David L. Brown/The Stock Market; p. 11: NASA/The Stock Market; p. 12: James Levin/Scholastic.

No part of this publication may be reproduced in whole or in part, or stored in a retrieval system, or transmitted in any form or by any means, electronic, mechanical, photocopying, recording, or otherwise, without written permission of the publisher. For information regarding permission, write to Scholastic Inc., 555 Broadway, New York, NY 10012.

Library of Congress Cataloging-in-Publication Data
Canizares, Susan, 1960-
Jobs/Susan Canizares, Betsey Chessen.
p.cm.--(Social studies emergent readers)
Summary: Simple text and photographs explore the different things people do in their jobs, including making things, growing things, and helping, as well as the one thing they all have in common.
ISBN 0-439-04551-7 (pbk.: alk. paper)
1. Occupations--Juvenile literature. 2. Professions--Juvenile literature.
[1. Occupations.] I. Chessen, Betsey, 1970-. II. Title. III. Series.
HF5381.2.C36 1998
331.7'02--dc21   98-54176
                                                                                                                  CIP AC

Copyright © 1999 by Scholastic Inc.
Illustrations copyright © 1999 by Scholastic Inc.
All rights reserved. Published by Scholastic Inc.
Printed in the U.S.A.

19 18 17 16 15 14 13   08   09 08 07 06

What do people do on the job?

Some people make things.

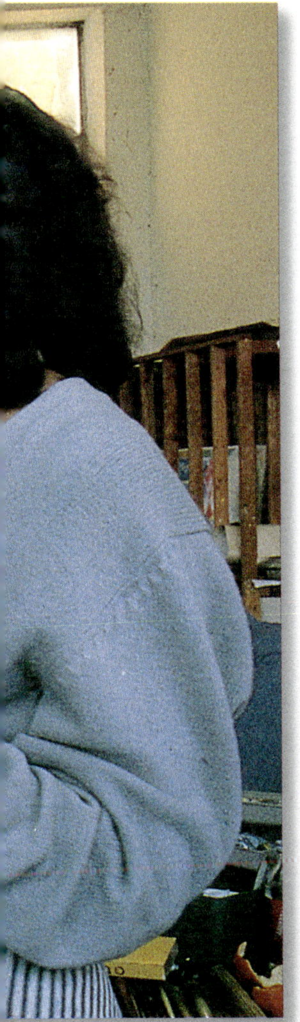

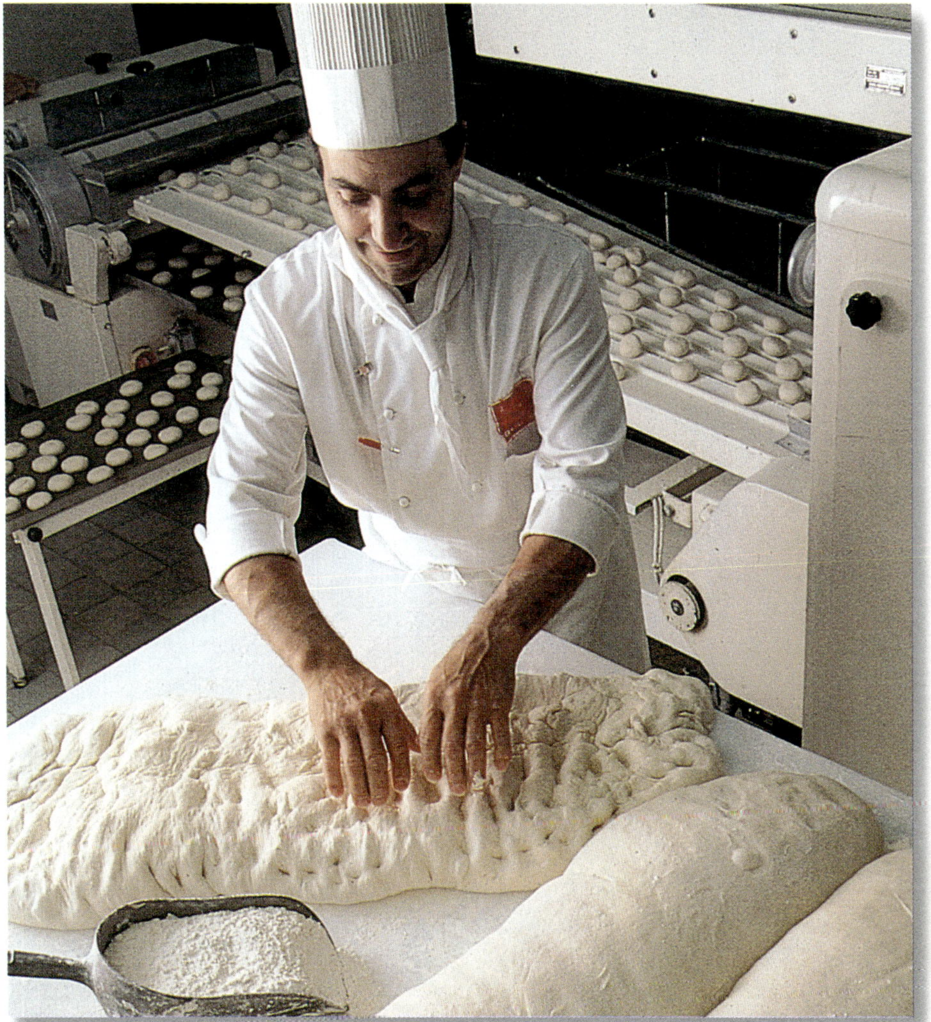

Other people build things.

Some people move things.

Other people grow things.

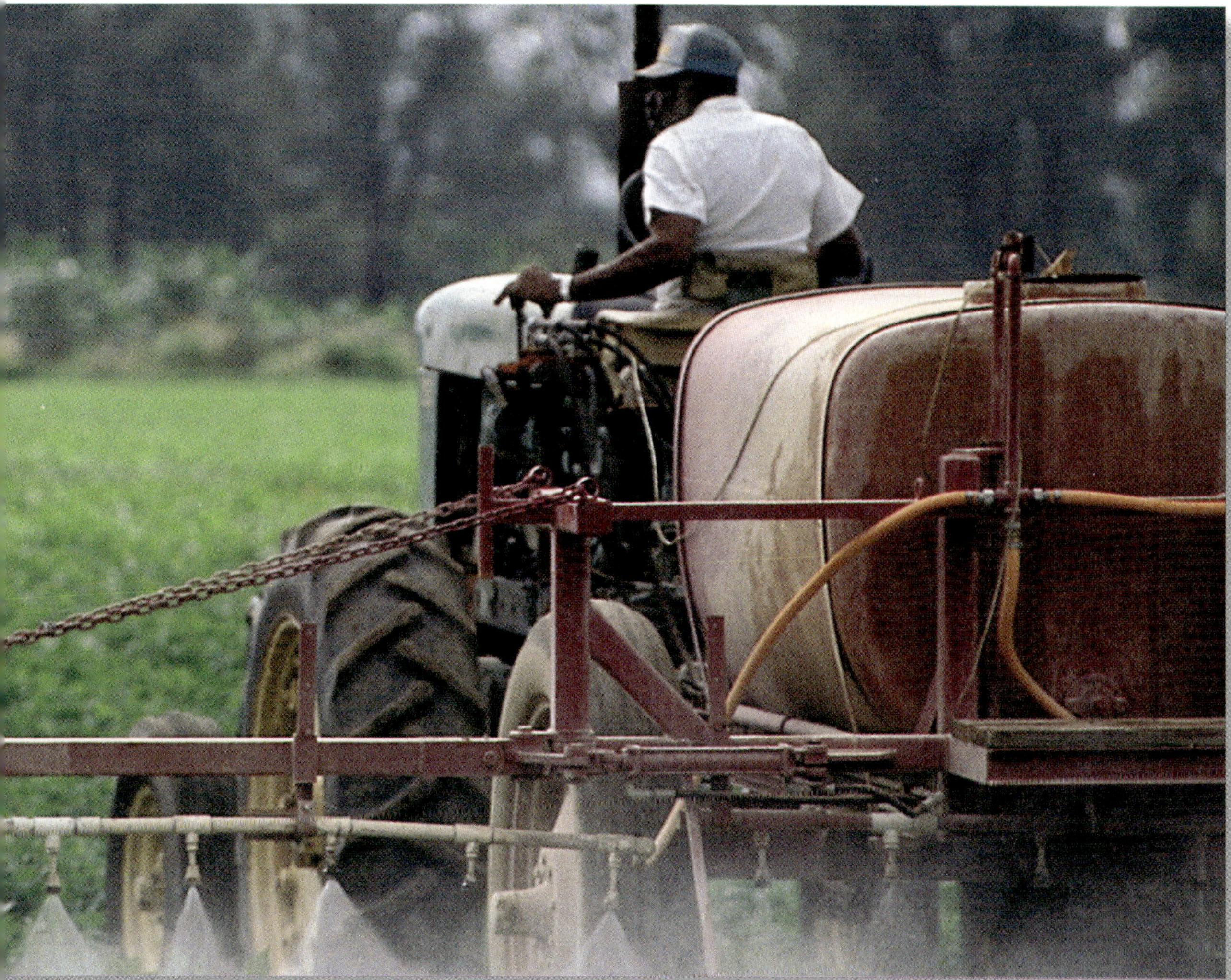

Some people help.

Other people heal.

People discover.

People explore.

On the job, everybody learns.

JOBS

People work to earn money for food, clothing, and shelter. But many people don't just choose jobs because of the money. People also choose jobs because they love doing certain activities, like making things or helping people.

Build It takes a lot of people to put up buildings. Surveyors measure and lay out the boundaries of the land. Architects design the buildings. Engineers do calculations to make sure the structure will stand. Masons do stonework, bricklayers put down bricks, and carpenters construct wood frames. Plumbers install pipes, and electricians put in wires for the lights. Still others put on the roof, build walls, plaster, and paint.

Move Moving things from place to place is an important job. Some people load trucks with produce, which truck drivers bring to its destination. Cargo handlers load things onto trains, ships, trucks, and planes. Then drivers or pilots carry these things all over the world. Other people, called movers, transport people's belongings when they move into a new house.

Make Things Lots of people's jobs involve making things. People like bakers or artists start with ingredients or raw materials or ideas. Then they work to make these things into finished products. Bakers make breads and cakes. Artists make paintings and sculptures. Authors make books and poems.

Grow Many people help to grow crops on today's big farms. Crops are plants that people consume, such as grains, fruits, vegetables, cotton, and rubber plants. Irrigation specialists know how to get the right amount of water to plants. Entomologists know all about insects and how to stop them from eating the plants, and seed producers create good seeds for planting.

Help Firefighters are at work, often risking their lives, to help save lives, property, and forests every day all over the world. The first thing they must do when they arrive at the scene of a fire is determine whether people need to be rescued. Then they fight the fire using three main methods: cooling (pumping water onto it), smothering (covering it with a layer of foam), and isolating (digging a trench that the fire can't cross).

Heal Nursing is one type of job in the healing professions. Nurses provide everyday care of patients, while medical doctors examine patients, make diagnoses, and decide on the treatment. Many doctors are specialists: pediatricians are children's doctors; surgeons perform operations; dentists take care of our teeth; and optometrists take care of our eyes. And let's not forget veterinarians, who take care of our pets.

Discover Archaeologists make discoveries by searching through ancient texts and digging through the soil to find things buried under the ground. Other people who discover things are astronomers, who look for new stars and life on other planets; historians, who discover information about our past; and scientists, who make discoveries that affect health and technology.

Explore Most of the earth has already been explored, so many explorers today are going into space and the ocean to discover new territory. Astronauts are space explorers. Yury Gagarin—a Russian and the first man in space—orbited the earth in 1961, and in 1969 Neil Armstrong walked on the moon. Undersea exploration is made possible by new diving equipment that can go deeper than ever before, allowing explorers to examine rocks, minerals, and sea life on the ocean floor.

Teach Forty-eight million people around the world are teachers. Pupils as well as teachers are constantly learning new things. However, teachers are not the only ones who learn from their jobs—everyone learns something on the job.

Social Studies
EMERGENT READERS

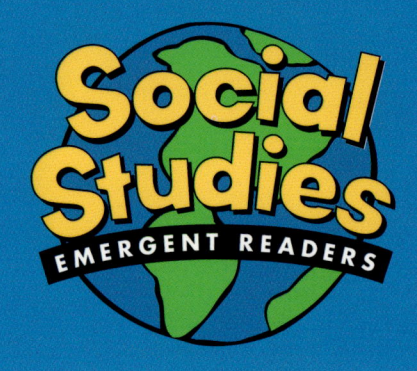

People do many different things on the job. Discover the one thing they all have in common.

ISBN 0-439-04551-7

Scholastic Inc.
$3.25 US